Barbie™ Exclusives

IDENTIFICATION & VALUES

BOOK II

FEATURING:
TOYS "Я" US
DOLLS OF THE WORLD
ASSORTED CUSTOMIZED DOLLS
& MATTEL'S FESTIVAL DOLLS

Margo Rana

COLLECTOR BOOKS
A Division of Schroeder Publishing Co., Inc.

～❦～

Cover design: Beth Summers
Book design: Joyce Cherry

Searching For A Publisher?

We are always looking for knowledgeable people considered to be experts within their fields. If you feel that there is a real need for a book on your collectible subject and have a large comprehensive collection contact Collector Books.

Additional copies of this book may be ordered from:

COLLECTOR BOOKS
P.O. Box 3009
Paducah, Kentucky 42002-3009

Margo's
3024 De La Vina St.
Santa Barbara, CA 93105
805–687–5677
orders only
Fax 805–569–0088

@$18.95. Add $2.00 for postage and handling.

Copyright: Margo Rana, 1996

Printed by IMAGE GRAPHICS, INC., Paducah, Kentucky

About the Author

In *Barbie Exclusives Book I* you saw Margo Rana with her first Barbie doll. It was Christmas morning in Orlando, Florida, 1959. Thirty-five years later Margo returned to Orlando to attend Mattel's Barbie Festival. Her Aunt Katy, seen on the right, picked her up at the airport and Margo had her drive by Toy Parade, the store in which her number 2 Barbie doll was purchased. Margo was sad to see that Toy Parade had closed some weeks before. As a child Margo would study the Barbie booklet, count her pennies, and decide between Busy Gal and Solo in the Spotlight fashions for Barbie. It took a long time to save up and then there was only enough money for one ensemble.

In the early '60s few children had more than one Barbie doll. They were expensive. In today's market this doll would probably retail for around $50. Few mothers will spend that kind of money on a doll for her children to play with. Children were taught to take care of their dolls. Mattel amazingly keeps the price down, so by the age of eight most little girls have at least 13 Barbie dolls and there are many more fashions for their dolls than were available in the 1959 catalog. Some things have changed, but the love for Barbie doll and her friends continues to grow.

Introduction

I am very pleased that so many of you have enjoyed my *Barbie Exclusives Identification and Values Guide, Book I.* I was ecstatic to hear that the first printing set a record by selling out in 30 days. The staff at Collector Books was on the ball. They recognized the demand and increased the first printing. When it was nearly sold out, they immediately started the second printing, so there was minimal lag time in filling orders.

I was relieved that you, the readers, did not beat me up while you had to wait for Book II. You all have been wonderfully patient, for which I thank you. Will you be as patient for Book III? Each book took a year to put together. It's a lot like waiting for our Barbie Dolls to come in from Mattel. There's great anticipation knowing it's coming; the anxiety of waiting for it to arrive and then the excitement of its arrival.

This time I am offering basically four different categories: Toys Я Us, The Dolls of the World, Customized Exclusives that have been released to date, and the Festival Dolls.

The first category is Toys Я Us. In many ways this book was easier to do than Book I, and in many ways it was more difficult. I never collected all the Toys Я Us Dolls. So, when it came time to do this book, I had to purchase most of them. They were easy to find and although most were on secondary market, they were not expensive. One of the things that made it easier was some new camera equipment that made my photo sessions to go faster with fewer re-shoots. Many of these dolls have fiber hair, and not being a stylist, I found it frustrating. I have to thank my good friend Carolyn for saving me from pulling out both my doll's hair and mine. She really is good. Just look at the dolls' hair; that's her work you see. She has the patience of a saint.

The second category, The Dolls of the World Collection, originally started in the customized division of Mattel. The early angled boxes were originally sold in better department stores. As time passed, Mattel realized that they could supply more collectors with these dolls if they opened up the market by offering them to specialty shops, and so they did.

In recent years, Mattel opened up sales of these dolls to anyone who had an account. Production levels are quite high now and Mattel keeps reissuing early releases. This has caused the resale market of early dolls in this category to relax. I have always considered the International Dolls to be a safe market. Under the circumstances, however, it is difficult to predict where the values will go with these dolls. After all these years I still enjoy the Dolls of the World immensely and will continue to build my collection because I love to look and play with them.

The third category I cover is a continuation of Book I, the harder-to-find customized dolls. Unfortunately, I could not get my hands on dolls that were not released at the time my deadline was due. I couldn't even get a list, so how could I get the dolls? Oh, well! The dolls I do picture are lovely.

The fourth category covers the Festival Dolls. In the fall of 1994, Mattel sponsored a spectacular event at the Contemporary, World Famous Disney Hotel in Orlando, Florida. Mattel and Disney threw a world class birthday party for Barbie. Mattel trucked in thousands and thousands of dollars worth of decorations, prototype dolls, thousands of yards of fabrics, staff members, and on and on and on. It was obvious that they spared no expense. Although there were some little problems here and there, the staff took on the Barbie motto, "We girls can do anything," and they did!

Some want to refer to the Festival as a convention. This is not correct. This phenomenon should only be termed "The Festival." I don't know if Mattel will ever have another one. But if they do, I'll be there! Hope to see you if they do.

A word on boxes; those of you who read Book I, know I don't care about boxes. Now I get to talk out of the other side of my mouth. There are some boxes I do care about. Gift set boxes, for example, are important to me, because without them there isn't any other way to prove that what you have is a gift set.

There are three basic box styles that Mattel uses. There is the book box, which opens just like a book. This is sometimes referred to as a hinged box. The second is a window box. These sometimes have cello windows which causes them to damage easily. They require special handling. If you feel the overwhelming urge to lift someone else's boxed doll, don't grab it by the cello! The chances are you will devaluate their doll by denting the plastic or putting a hole in it with your finger.

The third box is my favorite. It is a shoe box style. The lid comes completely off. In this way you have the opportunity to really see that special doll. If her hair is out of place or her skirt is flipped up you can actually fix it. The shoe box enables both box collector and doll collector to have what they want. If you are concerned about your doll getting dusty while on display, put the top of the box underneath and put some saran wrap over it.

The best box ever done was only used once to my knowledge and it was on the Applause Belle doll page 129. Here we have the best of both worlds. A shoe box and a window. If you like this too, I encourage you to write Mattel and tell them. Don't call their 800 number. That would just jam up the lines, and they're busy enough these days with collectors wondering where their dolls are.

Once again, I need to address values. Supply and demand. That is the equation that determines values. There has been an overwhelming influx of collectors even since Book I was released, and I predict that more will have joined our happy little group by the time this book hits the stands. The supply doesn't increase. So don't be surprised if you have to pay more for the doll you want than the price listed here.

And now some words of thanks. I want to thank Bob Gardner for sharing information as he did with Book I, and proofing my manuscript to make sure that all the information and facts I had gathered were correct. I am sorry to say that the Snow Princess pictured in this book belongs to Bob, not me. It is a treasure. He let me photograph it. He even let me touch it.

I also want to thank Joan Mitchell for dropping everything and staying up half the night editing my mistakes. I needed to meet my deadline and I appreciate her help.

I want to thank all the dealers across the country who gave Book I such great reviews and who sold it in their shops and at the shows. Last, but not least, all of you who have bought my books. I hope you enjoy my work, my photos, my dolls!

Sincerely,

Contents

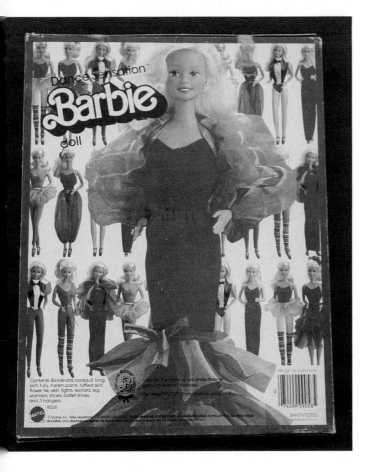

Dance Sensation #9058 • 1984 • $45.00

This is the first Toys Я Us customized Barbie doll. It wasn't just a doll, but a gift set too. All those great ensemble pieces to play with. Lavender eyes are not a common occurrence. I studied her face and said to myself, why is this so familiar? I immediately went to my '80s dolls to find the answer. Two years earlier, this doll was named Dream Date. You will see as you read on that some of these faces will repeat elsewhere. You might recognize the fashions as "spectacular fashions" from Mattel's 1983 regular line catalog.

Vacation Sensation Blue #1675 • 1986 • $60.00

Two years passed before Toys Я Us created another customized doll. Vacation Sensation was a regular line doll two years earlier. In 1984 she was named Day to Night. Here you see her re-dressed with a box filled with lots of accessories for Barbie doll to take on her vacation. It's as if the Day-to-Night Barbie doll got tired of working at the office and went on vacation.

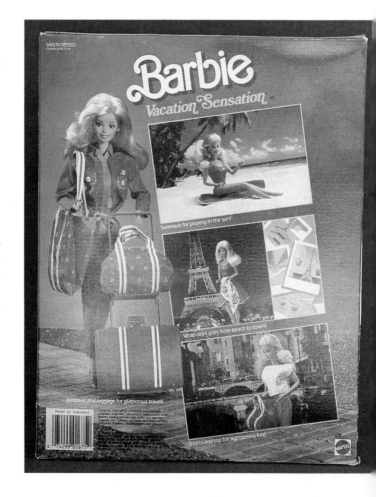

Vacation Sensation Pink #1675 • 1988 • $85.00

Another two years passed before we saw another
exclusive from Toys Я Us. This doll kept the same
name and same stock number. Both the content
and the package changed somewhat and the outfit
was pink, not blue. Mattel did not make many of
these gift sets in pink. In 1989 this exact face was
used for Walmart's Lavender Looks Barbie doll.
(See page 105 of *Barbie Exclusives, Book I.*)

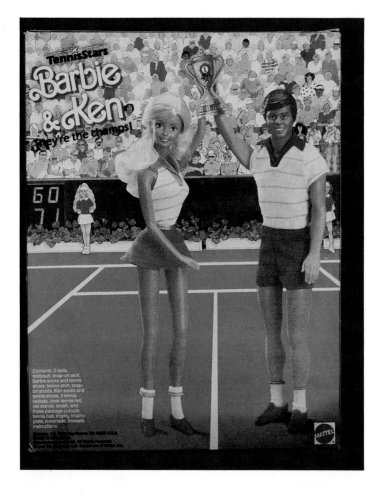

Tennis Stars Barbie & Ken #7801 • 1988 • $75.00

Tennis Stars Barbie and Ken dolls were the fourth customized gift set of Toys Я Us. I love the line! Barbie always draws a crowd of spectators, doesn't she? They're watching her every move. Notice Skipper doll's image on the back of the box. She was sold only in Europe. You could buy these dolls boxed individually in Canada, Mexico, and Europe.

Show 'n Ride #7799 • 1988 • $45.00

The year 1988 marked a tremendous influx of collectors. I attribute that to Mattel's smart decision to create the 1988 Holiday Barbie Doll. The Toys Я Us buying office must have recognized that Mattel was on to something here, because by 1989 Toys Я Us would contract for four customized Barbie dolls. Not all collectors had figured out that Toys Я Us had exclusives, because in 1990 you could still find Show 'N Ride on some shelves in some parts of the country. Show 'N Ride is one of my favorites. Almost simultaneously a riding outfit fashion was also available only in Europe. You see in the photo the first variation. Prancer the horse was sold separately. This simply painted face will appear again on page 88. This doll was identical to the 1988 Canadian doll from the Dolls of the World Collection, which back then could be purchased only in your better stores.

Party Treats #4885 • 1989 • $20.00

There isn't much to say about Party Treats Barbie doll. Mine must have been made on a Friday because her hair is a fright. She was considerably less expensive than her customized predecessors. She makes a good gift for the money. I got a phone call one day from a customer who had received this doll and was concerned because the doll's head was bent backwards and looking up to heaven. I told him it's a great bottom shelf doll. If you have a doll like that, don't put her on the top shelf because you can't see her face. If you place her on the bottom shelf she's looking up to you. The reverse is true if you have a doll looking down, put her on the top shelf, so you get to see her face.

Ready for party fun!

Pepsi Spirit Barbie #4869 • 1989 • $100.00

Here Mattel licensed with Pepsi and came up with a cute kicky ensemble for Barbie doll. The box says she's dressed for Pepsi fun, and what's in the duffel bag? It must be to hold her matching Pepsi beach towel!

Pepsi Spirit Skipper #4867 • 1989 • $85.00

Pepsi Skipper doll's checkerboard sox match Barbie doll's bag. Off to the beach they go for more of that Pepsi fun. Skipper doll has her own Pepsi bag and beach towel and a change of clothes, again with the matching logo. Too bad they didn't have a soda shop to match.

Cool City Blues Gift Set #4893 • 1989 • $75.00

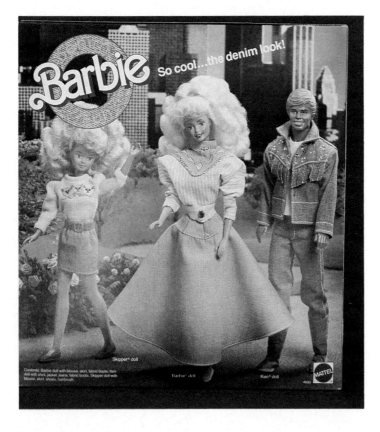

Cool City Blues gift set includes Barbie, Ken, and Skipper. Their fashions were sold separately in 1988 at all toy stores. This was Toys Я Us' first three-doll package. Here we have another familiar Barbie doll face. In 1990, this Barbie doll changed her clothes and went to Children's Palace as a Mouseketeer. Cool City Blues Barbie doll's bangs are a bit longer and are wrapped with a rubber band. You might be fooled at first, so look closely at the face on page 16 in *Barbie Exclusives, Book I.* Cool City Blues Barbie doll's arms are straight, Mouseketeer Barbie doll's are bent. Ken is one of the many Malibu dolls, and Skipper has a mound of curls that would make Shirley Temple jealous.

Sweet Roses #7635 • 1989 • $50.00

Sweet Roses Barbie is the same doll as Home Pretty Barbie, which was featured in Mattel's 1990 regular line catalog. This doll was designed to go with the fabulous Magical Mansion. The suggested retail price on the Mansion was $500.00. Needless to say, Mattel sold more Sweet Roses dolls than homes. They do belong together, however.

Cool Looks #5947 • 1990 • $25.00

Cool Looks Barbie wanted to support her little sister in business, so she bought her new summer outfit from Skipper doll's t-shirt shop. Notice that the bag my doll is carrying is not the same one that Mattel photographed for the box. You'll remember from *Barbie Exclusives, Book* I that the art work is often done before the final product and there can be changes before the doll is actually produced. Changes can be for any number of reasons; supplies not available and customer request are the most common reasons.

Winter Fun #5949 • 1990 • $45.00

Fur-trimmed dolls in elegant attire are among the most popular dolls that Mattel produces. Somehow the fur-trimmed sportswear dolls often get overlooked. Or should I say, underestimated? Winter Fun Barbie and Ski Fun Midge dolls are the only customized fur-trimmed dolls for Toys Я Us.

Ski Fun Midge #7513 • 1991 • $40.00

Best friends do more than play Barbie and comb Barbie doll's hair. They go skiing together, too. Barbie and Midge are outfitted in chic ski attire. For once Midge doll doesn't have to borrow clothes from Barbie doll. Offered separately was their own ski lodge, as pictured on the back of Midge doll's box. This doll was sold as a regular line doll in Europe and Canada. Not shown is Snow Dancer, Midge doll's horse, which was a Toys Я Us exclusive. Snow Dancer was available at all stores in Europe and Canada.

Dream Date Skipper #1075 • 1990 • $30.00

Does the name Dream Date sound familiar to you? If it does it's because in 1982 we had Dream Date Barbie, Ken, and PJ dolls. I think those dolls were great. This Skipper doll, however, has no relationship as far as I can tell to the older dolls. Her flocked illusion skirt has more in common with Walmart's Frills and Fantasy as seen in *Barbie Exclusives, Book I* on page 104. To see Skipper doll with strawberry blonde hair and a hairpiece is quite unique. This doll was also available as a regular line doll for the European market.

Western Fun Gift Set #5408 • 1990 • $75.00

Barbie doll and Sun Runner lead the parade at the State Fair in 1990. Barbie doll selected a Barbie-pink and turquoise, Santa Fe inspired ensemble for this event. She selected matching accessories for her favorite palomino, Sun Runner. Western Fun dolls could be purchased separately at local stores. This gift set was exclusive to Toys Я Us and the wholesale clubs.

Beauty Pageant Skipper #9324 • 1991 • $30.00

Of the many Skipper dolls over the years, this is my favorite of the newer releases. It's that derby! It's not shown here but it is included in the package. Skipper doll wears it for the talent portion of the beauty pageant. Beauty Pageant Skipper doll was available as part of the regular line in Europe.

Totally Hair Skipper #1430 • 1991 • $30.00

The bestselling doll of all time for Mattel was Totally Hair Barbie. Toys Я Us was the only company to offer Totally Hair Skipper and Courtney dolls. Dressed to accent Barbie and Ken doll's attire in 1960s Emilio Pucci-type printed fabric, Skipper with her fabulously long crimped hair is cute as can be.

Totally Hair Courtney #1433 • 1991 • $30.00

It was thoughtful of Mattel to see to it that Skipper had a little friend to go to the beauty salon with. I'm sure they had their hair crimped together. Here we see Courtney doll mimicking Skipper doll's every move. Little known Totally Hair Whitney doll was sold in Europe only. (Whitney doll is not shown.)

Spring Parade #7008 • 1991 • $40.00

This doll has a southern belle feeling to her. She would fit in well with Sears "Southern Belle." The flowers in her bag are the same as those we saw in Sweet Spring's straw bag. (See page 84 of *Barbie Exclusives, Book 1.*)

Spring Parade #2257 •1991 • $35.00

Neither the white Spring Parade doll nor the black doll sold well for Toys Я Us, so the following Easter season, special labels were made promoting her as the "perfect gift to put in an Easter basket." Her lack of popularity keeps her value low. This black version is difficult to get. Notice that she was packaged in the white doll's box and little stickers were made to cover the white doll's stock number with a different number.

School Fun # 2721 • 1991 • $25.00

Mattel has had many school themed dolls in recent years. They are often released in August to coordinate with September school registrations. This is a dual marketing strategy that's almost subtle. As mothers and daughters go shopping for back-to-school clothes and book supplies, what better time to market a school-oriented doll?

School Fun #4111 • 1991 • $25.00

Barbie doll's outfit is complete with letterman's jacket. That's what those of us who grew up in the '50s call them. Barbie doll comes complete with book bag and two pencils with no erasers. Barbie doesn't need erasers, she never makes a mistake! I, on the other hand wrote this book in pencil and bought extra erasers.

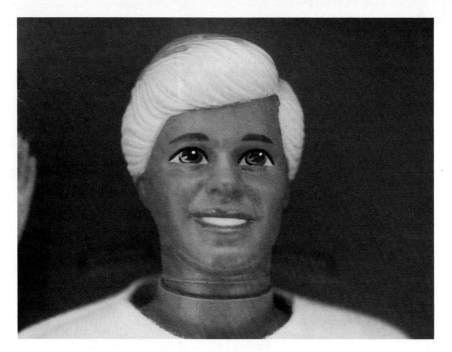

Barbie & Friends Gift Set #3177 • 1991 • $75.00

Those Mouseketeer ears did well for the Heart family dolls and for Children's Palace Barbie — so naturally we can assume that it did well for Toys Я Us. Each doll in this three-doll gift set had a special Disney t-shirt to wear to the park. Ken doll wears Mickey, Barbie doll wears Minnie, and Skipper doll wears Donald Duck. The shirts were special just for these dolls. Barbie doll's face is gorgeous. What can you say, there's that Malibu face mold for Ken doll again. And Skipper doll looks like she's had a little too much cotton candy. There was a two doll gift set made for Euro Disney two years later. Although the dolls were different, the clothing they wore was identical.

Barbie For President #3722 • 1991 • $100.00/$50.00

Although Barbie For President was not billed as the first in the "Career Collection," Geralyn Nelson, the designer of this doll, has assured me it is. In a presidential campaign year, what better theme than this to follow "we girls can do anything?" There was just one little snafu. The only one who has the honor of utilizing the presidential seal is the president him/herself. There were two versions of her box. The first one bore the Seal of the President of the United States. Since Barbie doll had not officially won the election, Mattel had to take the privilege away from her. Production of the packaging ceased and a star was put in its place. There were fewer boxes with the seals, consequently commanding greater value.

Barbie For President #3940 • 1991 • $50.00

To the best of my knowledge no black Barbie doll's package ever reached the market place with the presidential seal. This indicates that the situation was discovered before the packaging for black Barbie doll went into production. These dolls were a hit with both Democrats and Republicans. Although Barbie doll claimed no particular party, she campaigned in her Nancy Reagan red suit and attended the inaugural ball in appropriate red, white, and blue. Even though she lost the right to display the presidential seal, in this gown she was a winner all the way. P.S. she looks great on display with an entourage from the UNICEF collection.

Wedding Day Kelly & Todd #2820 • 1991 • $45.00

Midge and Alan finally decided to get married. Mattel offered the specialty shops a six doll gift set. The 11½" dolls were offered individually in the regular line division and the little ones were packaged as a set only at Toys Я Us. Throughout the group there were lots of variations, from Midge doll's rare hair color to the lace trims. Here we have some obvious variations on Kelly: different lace trims, larger swiss dot; the flowers in one are satin, the other is something else; the fluff in the basket of one is illusion, the other is chiffon; one Kelly has glossy lips, the other has dull. Now compare them to the back of the box. Mattel claims this to be a Toys Я Us exclusive, but it could also be bought through J.C. Penney's catalog if you bought both Midge and Alan. It was billed as J.C. Penney's four-doll gift set.

Sweet Romance #2917 • 1991 • $30.00

Sweet Romance Barbie doll wears fabric that reminds me of Spectra as well as Magic Moves Barbie. Her shiny lamé is the selling point on this doll. She's gorgeous in her sophisticated ice blue satin gown.

Malt Shoppe #4581 • 1992 • $35.00

This is one of the cutest concepts Anne Bray in the design department has put together, or maybe it's just my nostalgic feelings showing through. This is what I would wear when I played with my #2. For those fortunate enough to have Barbie doll's '57 Chevy, it makes a fun display.

Fashion Brights #1882 • 1992 • $25.00

Fashion Brights Barbie doll is an inexpensive straight armed doll that would make a great gift for any little girl. This gift set came with numerous fashion pieces to play with. The retail price on this gift set was a minimal investment for lots of play time for the children.

Fashion Brights #4112 •1992 • $25.00

Here we have the black version with all the components as the white gift set. The bra and pantie shown on the box is the same fabric used on one of the slim box dolls from the regular line.

Cool 'N Sassy #1490 • 1992 • $25.00

Any doll with her lingerie hanging out couldn't be anything else but sassy! I'm not so sure about the cool part.

Cool 'N Sassy #4110 • 1992 • $25.00

Maybe little girls are wearing their undergarments on top of their clothing and maybe Madonna looks good that way to some. But I'm sorry! I'm just old fashioned and just hate seeing this encouraged. Once I get past all that, this doll isn't so bad.

Radiant in Red #1276 • 1992 • $75.00

We saw only a few red-haired dolls in the '80s and early '90s in the Dolls of the World Series. When Geralyn Nelson designed this Titian doll for Toys R Us they immediately had a success on their hands. As the first in the series, she should command the greater value, but I have a hunch that the Purple Passion will give her a run for the money. The first red-haired department store special was in 1971; Hair Happenin's Barbie doll.

Radiant in Red #4113 • 1992 • $75.00

Unfortunately this photo does not do this doll justice. She is gorgeous! I prefer her to the white version. They both seem to sell equally well. If you don't have her in your collection, think about her again, and soon. I predict that the value above will not stay this low for very long.

❦ ❦ ❧

Love-to-Read #10507 • 1992 • $50.00

I had fun with this gift set. In 1992 I was invited to display some of my dolls at the Santa Barbara Public Library. I featured this doll in the center of the showcase with many vintage Barbie books. Somehow it slipped by the librarian. I had to point it out. Actually, I'm sure she would have figured it out, the display was pretty awesome for a small town and maybe there was too much to see. Anne Bray was the designer of Love to Read.

❦ ❦ ❧

Quinceañera Teresa #11928 • 1994 • $30.00

The most mispronounced doll Mattel has made, phonetically, kenn - seen - yare - ah. Living in an Hispanic community helps with this tongue twister. Quinceañera is a Hispanic birthday celebration, similar to a Bar Mitzvah or coming-out party. At the age of 15 a party is thrown for the young ladies. The birthday girl chooses 15 of her best friends to dress up as her attendants and the festival lasts all day. Geralyn Nelson created this special occasion doll for us.

In her glittery evening dress,
Police Officer Barbie
shines with pride at the
Police Awards Ball. Everyone
applauds as she receives the
Best Police Officer Award
for her courageous
acts in the community.

Safety tips, a police dog, "walkie-talkie,"
award and "flashlight" for Barbie!
(Cut-outs included inside.)

Doll cannot stand alone.   10688

Police Officer #10688 • 1993 • $75.00

Second in the career collection of Toys Я Us
this doll has been as big a hit as her predecessor. Geralyn Nelson was inspired to design this
doll because of her husband's occupation. Barbie doll's hat and badge bear her husband's
number. Who should be more honored? He or
Barbie doll? Barbie doll teaches safety tips to
grade schoolers. She comes with several accessories as seen on the box, as well as a cocktail
dress to wear to the Best Police Officers Award
Banquet.

Police Officer #10688 • 1993 • $75.00

Police Officer Barbie doll wears her badge #77 with pride. She comes with a shield, night stick, walkie talkie, and K-9... all made from the highest grade cardboard. Do you think we'll see a K-9 patrol car for her in the future? Wouldn't that be cute? It's too bad Harley Davidson didn't go for Mattel's proposal to produce their motorcycle, that would have been fun, too.

School Spirit #10682 • 1993 • $30.00

The minute you turn around it's back to school...no other way to go than with lots of spirit. Barbie doll is planning to go to the big game on Saturday. Her fabric may look familiar to you. It is the same fabric as we see on Beach Fun Barbie and Ken gift set from the wholesale club that same year. (See page 137 in *Barbie Exclusives, Book I.*)

School Spirit #10683 • 1993 • $25.00

In the 1960s the letter of choice was "M" for Mattel not "B" as you see here on Barbie doll's jacket. She comes with a backpack and two pencils.

Spots 'n Dots #10491 • 1993 • $45.00

I don't know why I didn't snap this doll up when she was first released. I liked her and I left her. I recently bought her from another dealer. I kicked myself till I got her out of the box...don't tell the other shop keeper, but knowing how great she is, I would have paid more. Do you think Barbie doll put on this darling little frock just to walk her dog? We saw this Dalmatian with the Career Girl three-fashion gift set and again with Fire Fighter Barbie.

Spots 'n Dots Teresa #10885 • 1993 • $55.00

Here's Teresa doll wearing Barbie doll's dress and walking Barbie doll's dog. Note the nice saran hair. Ann Driskill is credited with designing both these appropriately named Spots' n Dots dolls.

Moonlight Magic #10608 • 1993 • $80.00

For this doll Mattel used fiber hair. The minut
you take her out of the box that darn hair goe
limp. It is my greatest disappointment with thes
dolls. Carolyn has saved the day for me b
restyling her hair so Moonlight Magic would b
presentable for her photo shoot.

Moonlight Magic #10609 • 1993 • $60.00

Ann Driskill chose rich looking fabric for Moonlight Magic Barbie doll. She looks fantastic on display with Service Merchandise's City Sophisticate. Considering how many dolls Mattel makes in the course of a year few are done in black fabric. However, we have seen more black in the last few years than ever before.

Dream Wedding Gift Set #10712 • 1993 • $65.00

The only thing missing from this picture is the groom. That Ken! Can anyone tell me, how many Barbie brides there have been with no groom? Isn't Barbie doll's face just perfect? She looks really happy.

Dream Wedding Gift Set #10713 • 1993 • $55.00

We always make fun of Ken not showing up for th
wedding. I have never heard anyone ask the wher
abouts of Mom and Dad. I called Mattel this mornir
and suggested they create them. With all this talk
family values, now is the marketing time for just th
concept. It would make great Mother and Father's d
gifts.

≈ ᢢ ᢢ

Party Time Barbie #12243 • 1994 • $24.00

I must own nine or ten Barbie doll watches and now I have two more just by purchasing these dolls. This makes for a good value. Even Barbie gets her own watch. Being on time is commendable; especially now that Barbie doll has all these careers at Toys Я Us. Heather Dutton designed both these Party Time dolls. Recently Mattel produced a black version exclusively for Toys Я Us.

Party Time Teresa #12244 • 1994 • $24.00

I'm really glad to see that Mattel gave Teresa doll her own dress. If you don't like crimped hair, comb her fiber hair and I promise her wave will go away.

Astronaut #12149 • 1994 • $80.00

Amazing, it's only been four years and this is Barbie doll's third career. She was an Astronaut back in 1965 and again in 1985 and for the third time in her 35 years in 1994. Her accessories are similar to those in the 1985; version: uniform, helmet, boots. Newly added is the glow in the dark moon rocks. Susan Davis of Space Week has confirmed that the real moon rocks don't glow.

Astronaut #12150 • 1994 • $60.00

Once a year NASA celebrates Space
Week. 1994 marked the 25th Anniversary of the Apollo moonwalk. In 1969
everything shut down and we were all
glued to our TVs. July 20th is the day we
celebrate Neil Armstrong and Dr. Buzz
Aldrin's famous walk on the moon. If you
want to know more, call the number on
the box. Chances are you'll get to talk to
Susan Davis who has all the Apollo II
answers.

Emerald Elegance #12322 • 1994 • $55.00

Collectors have been clamoring for years, wanting
more Barbie dolls with hair color other than
blonde. It seems that Radiant 'n Red was so suc-
cessful that Toys Я Us and Mattel decided to repeat
a good thing. If my doll's hair looks different than
yours it's because Carolyn had to restyle her fiber
hair for this picture.

Emerald Elegance #12323 • 1994 • $55.00

Barbie doll's satin gown with lace overlay at the last minute had a name change. She was originally offered to another company, which ended up selecting another doll for their store. Once again, Geralyn Nelson designed a great doll.

Sunflower Barbie #13488 • 1994 • $25.00

This special edition for Toys Я Us is too adorable! Sunflowers are extremely popular right now with decorators, flower growers, and Mattel. She's available at the time of this writing, but I don't expect her to be around long. I'm proud to say I needed no assistance in combing her hair for this picture. Mattel selected a great saran-like fiber to put under that perky little hat.

Sunflower Teresa #13489 • 1994 • $45.00

I get reports from all over the country and it seems that Teresa is scarce territorially speaking. If you have a hard time finding her, don't be surprised. The bodice on this doll is the same fabric used on the Disney Fun Barbie doll that was available only in Europe or specialty shops.

❧ ❦ ❧

Asha I #13532 • 1994 • $24.00

A couple years back Mattel featured in their regular line catalog a series of black dolls we refer to as the Shani collection. There were three in all, Asha, Nichelle, and Shani. Later came Jamal, the male counterpart. They are the best 11½" African-American dolls to hit the shelves.

❧ ❦ ❧

Asha II #12676 • 1994 • $24.00

This is the second Asha in the series for Toys Я Us. The fabric is referred to as kente cloth. This was the preferred cloth of western African royalty. You can see that a great deal of research went into the production of this doll. This is the same print as used on the first Asha on the opposite page. Try putting these dolls on display with your Kenyan and Nigerian dolls and build a beautiful display. Makes me wish I had saved a set of animals from Animal Lovin' Barbie from a couple of years ago.

Wedding Party Gift Set #13557 • 1994 • $40.00

I have never been a Bride collector. The only Brides
have in my own collection are Empress, the ra
haired porcelain, the rare haired Midge Weddi
Party, and the 1964 Wedding Day Gift Set. Conside
ing Mattel in recent times does no less than tv
brides a year that is not a lot of brides for one to ha
in a collection. This deluxe bride gift set is maki
me think I'll have to have another one. She is rea
lovely. Maybe it's because this is the gown I wou
choose for myself or maybe it's because I like th
saran hair, or maybe it's the way they painted h
face. At any rate, she is nice and I do like her.

Fire Fighter #13553 • 1994 • $35.00

Fourth in the Career Collection series is Fire Fighter Barbie doll. The year before Mattel offered a fashion gift set that included a fire fighter's outfit along with a teacher's outfit and a veterinarian's uniform. The fireman's outfit shown here is a bit different than the one in the fashion gift set.

Fire Fighter #13553 • 1994 • $30.00

Little Sparkey is too cute. She's waiting for her master's instructions. Every year the local fire department comes round to my store for an inspection. I had bought the fashion just to entertain them when they got here. We'll have more fun this year, because now I have three fire fighters.

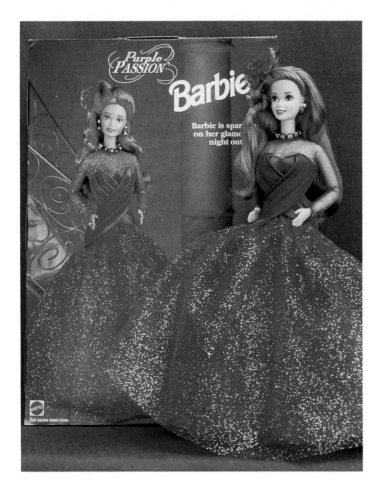

Purple Passion #13555 • 1995 • $30.00

This doll is gorgeous. Fourth in the series for Toys Я Us you can see that she was well thought out, well planned and designed. Here's not only the fourth doll but the third red head in the series. The carnival glass beads reflect all the colors in Barbie doll's eyes, lips, dress, and hair.

Purple Passion #13554 • 1995 • $35.00

Notice once again the beads. See how the carnival glass reflects so differently on this doll. It's the hair color that changes the reflection. Both the white doll and the black doll are two dolls you won't want to miss. Both Purple Passion dolls have beautiful saran locks.

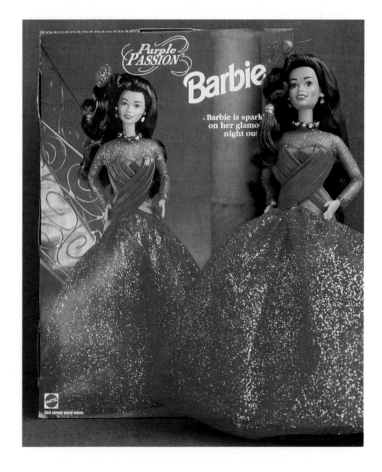

Sapphire Dream #13255 • 1995 • $125.00

Sapphire Dream is wonderful, with her rooted eyelashes, midnight blue velvet gown, and flowing chiffon cape. Barbie doll's hips look a little full in this fabric, but so would mine. The only thing that would have made me happier would be a better grade hair. This is one of few dolls I will leave in the box, only because you are looking at a sample. I may have to buy a second one to take out and play with. This is the first doll of the new higher priced Toys Я Us exclusives series Society Style Collection.

Dolls of the World

Royal #1601 • 1979 • $225.00

Three dolls were introduced in 1980 that woul
change the course of Barbie doll collecting for yea
to come. This line of dolls was introduced to bett
department stores. Every box would be filled wi
interesting information about each of the countri
Barbie doll represented. Each doll had her ow
stand, brochure, hair brush, and warranty paper
Up until 1992 each doll's box had a map of th
particular country. Here we have Royal Barbie dc
representing England. This is a reminder, that tl
dates at the top are box dates, not necessarily tl
date the dolls were released, nor the date on tl
doll.

Italian #1602 • N/A • $275.00

A unique face mold was used for the Italian doll. This mold has never again been used for production of a Barbie doll. This face mold was originally created for the Sunspell doll of the Guardian Goddesses produced by Mattel in 1977. Is this the mold they broke? She is the most difficult of the Dolls of the World to find, so if you don't have her, and you see her, buy her. Don't waffle, don't quibble, just buy her. The Italian Barbie doll was offered in Europe wearing the fashion sold in the United States known as Collector Series II, Springtime Magic.

Parisian #1600 • 1979 • $200.00

Parisian Barbie doll appropriately attired in France's classic cancan costume. Her green eyes and strawberry blonde hair make her particularly unusual. Parisian Barbie doll's eyes are the only ones I'm familiar with that have a starburst design.

Oriental #3262 • 1980 • $195.00

Oriental Barbie doll was originally styled with a flip style similar to the '69 twist and turn doll. She was shown in the 1981 Mattel department store division catalog with open toe slip-on shoes. The final product was released with T-straps and her hair was straightened. Mattel's logo for 1981 was "Your Partners in Profit."

Scottish #3263 • 1980 • $195.00

I bought this boxless Scottish doll
from a young lady who unfortunately
had the doll in the sunlight, consequently her dress is faded. I don't
mind, because this is the prettiest
face I've seen on a Scottish doll, and
that's more important to me than the
fact she came with no box.

India #3897 • 1982 • $195.00

This India doll is the only one that is part of the Dolls of the World series. There have been others that have been available in recent years that were made for distribution in India only by the Leo Corporation owned by Mattel. In the USA, the only way to get the Leo dolls were from specialty shops or shows.

Eskimo #3898 • 1991 • $175.00

The Oriental face mold that we got to see the year before is put to good use again on our Eskimo. It must be a good mold because Mattel keeps using it. Barbie doll's parka keeps her nice and toastie in the Alaskan cold. Mattel selected the Superstar face mold, gave her black hair and the same fashion as you see here, and produced an Eskimo doll for the Scandinavian countries (not shown, unfortunately).

Spanish #4031 • 1982 • $175.00

Spanish Barbie doll's costume is the classic flamenco dress. This particular doll represents Spain's capital of Madrid. You will see in the reissue another part of the country represented. Teresa doll's face mold, as you see here, will change. (See page 98.)

Swedish #4032 • 1982 • $150.00

Mattel designers study the countries, the geography, and especially the attire. The variation you see on page 118 isn't the result of a correction, but rather the shortage of fabric. I'm afraid I don't know which fabric came first, as I only found the variation about two years ago.

Irish #7517 • 1983 • $175.00

Barbie doll's green eyes get a lot of attention with her green satin shawl to enhance them. Barbie doll's hair has only a hint of red. This doll was also reissued. (See page 109.) Every year Mattel created a logo and proudly displays it on the cover of that year's department store special catalog. In 1983 the logo was "Mattel Delivers." That was a long time ago.

Swiss #5598 • 1983 • $135.00

Swiss Barbie doll's skirt and vest is of velveteen and the blouse of cotton. Barbie doll's hat is the same as the one on the Italian, just trimmed with different colors. In 1964 Mattel offered a fashion called Barbie in Switzerland (see page 94 of *Barbie Fashion* by Sarah Sink Eames). You will see that they are very different.

Japanese #9481 • 1984 • $175.00

Japanese Barbie is the doll most requested of me in the Dolls of the World collection. In spite of the overwhelming number of requests on this doll, her price remains stable. She is extremely popular. The interest in this doll is not limited to Dolls of the World collectors. Mattel had made a Japanese fashion for the American market in 1964 (see page 92 of *Barbie Fashions* by Sarah Sink Eames). There have been many kimono garbed dolls for the Orient, but this is the nicest.

Peruvian #2995 • 1985 • $125.00

As one of the more brightly colored ensembles for this series, this doll representing Peru is one I really like. The PJ face mold, with her whispering lips, is a collector favorite. Barbie doll's hat is made of felt and trimmed with festive flowers. This South American Indian represents the Incas.

Greek #2997 • 1985 • $100.00

Greek Barbie doll is wearing a moire skirt, halter, and velveteen jacket. Her gold braided tassel adds just enough color to make sure she gets your attention.

German #3188 • 1986 • $150.00

Many people like to buy the dolls that reflect their heritage. Because there are so many Germans here in the U.S. this doll sells extremely well. Barbie doll's jacket is the same fabric as you see on the Canadian (page 97) and on Show 'n Ride (page 14). I absolutely love the fabric of her hat! Wouldn't that have made a spectacular gown for a doll?

Icelandic #3189 • 1986 • $125.00

Here we have another velveteen
dressed doll. She has a gold string
vest closure, blouse, and satin apron.
Like the Peruvian doll, her hat is
made out of felt. It is a different style.
It would have to be to accommodate
her braided pigtails. This is the third
doll in this series to have pigtails.

Korean #4929 • 1987 • $125.00

This face mold that started out being referred to as the Oriental face mold is often referred to today as the Kira face mold. Her gown appears to be one piece, but it's not. She has a removable jacket. It's satin from head to toe, accented with gold trim. Simple elegance.

Canadian #4928 • 1987 • $100.00

Our friends and neighbors to the north were just as happy as we were to see this charming doll. Dressed in her work uniform Barbie doll is truly ready to get her man. Only this time it's men. It shouldn't be difficult for her lookin' so cute. Keeping in mind that this is the same face mold as you saw on page 14, Show 'n Ride Barbie doll from Toys Я Us.

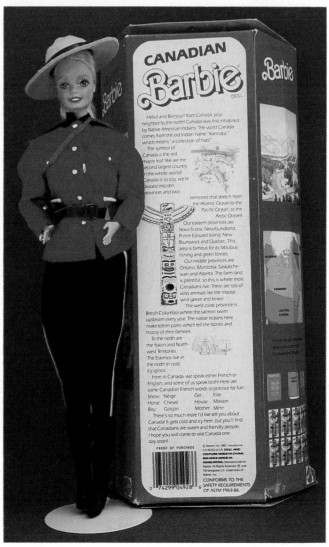

Mexican #1917 • 1988 • $75.00

Barbie doll had gone to Mexico back in 1964, as a fashion (see page 93 *Barbie Fashions* by Sarah Sink Eames). The patterns are similar. These dolls were extremely plentiful in states that border Mexico. They were available for a long time. Due to the length of time she was around, and a large supply, her value remained low for quite some time. She has just recently taken an increase in value, so if you haven't gotten one yet, do so before the price goes up again.

Russian #1916 • 1988 • $125.00

Russian Barbie doll is only the second fur-trimmed doll in the series. Her floor length dress will help keep her warm during those long winter months in her native country. The Soviet Union is one of two countries represented in the series that no longer exist. Her ensemble conjures up visions of *Dr. Zhivago*.

Brazilian #9094 • 1989 • $75.00

This makes the third doll from our neighbors south of the border. Barbie doll's two-piece dance ensemble is hot, hot, hot. Her drop waistband and hat are trimmed with the same print we saw on F.A.O Schwarz's Rockette page 38, Woolworth's Sweet Lavender on page 153, Star Dream, and Etoile du Patin, page 64, *Barbie Exclusives Book I.*

Nigerian #7376 • 1989 • $75.00

Nigerian Barbie is the first black doll in the grouping. She did not sell well at first, and she is hard to find today. This is another one whose price makes no sense. I predict that this will change. I can find no other doll wearing these gold pearled open toe sling backs. Very unusual color.

Eskimo Reissue #9844 • 1990 • $75.00

You can't please all the people all of the time. Many collectors are unhappy to see reissued dolls. With so many other countries in the world to be represented, I have trouble with that, too. On the other hand, not everyone's budget will allow them the opportunity to have the originals. In the end, they aren't identical, so have some fun with this.

≈ ✦ ≈

Parisian Reissue #9843 • 1990 • $85.00

The dress on this Parisian Barbie doll is almost identical to the first. Even her hair has the same upswept do. Her eyeshadow and eyeliner are perfect with her hair piece. This was the first doll from the series to be released in Japan with Japanese writing on the box.

≈ ✦ ≈

Malaysian #7329 • 1990 • $75.00

This doll was made out of the same plastic tone as we saw on the first Singapore Girl doll. (See *Barbie Exclusives, Book I* page 77.) Remember how I told you she didn't sell well? Well neither did this doll. I attribute it to that pale skin tone. Her dress is very *King and I*, and as popular as that movie was, I'm surprised that this wasn't enough to make up the difference.

Scottish Reissue #9845 • 1990 • $75.00

Scottish Barbie doll is lots of fun. I really enjoy the variation and reissue combination. The metallic threads in her ensemble give this doll just the lift she needs. In the photo you see two variations of the reissue. The original is on page 84 and a comparison photo on page 124.

❦ ✿ ❧

Czechoslovakian #7330 • 1990 • $150.00

Try spelling that one with your eyes closed. This doll was not very appreciated when she was first released, so Mattel cut production on her. No one wanted her. I don't understand why. She's really cute. The fabric is great, so why the resistance? Her hair appears to be braided, but it's not. It's twisted with her red ribbon. The boots are right out of the '70s. When collectors realized they didn't have all the Dolls of the World, it was too late for this one. She was gone and now you'll have to pay! Maybe this year you'll order your dolls early.

❦ ✿ ❧

Spanish Reissue #4963 • 1991 • $55.00

Our first Spanish doll hailed from Madrid. This reissue is wearing a costume from the city of Cataluyna. Barbie doll's mantilla is extremely full. She comes with a red comb, which I couldn't get to stay in her hair. It doesn't matter, because I prefer the mantilla.

Jamaican #4647 • 1991 • $55.00/$75.00

You may be saying to yourself, the earrings on the standing doll look silver, and the earrings on the close-up look blue. Well, you're absolutely right. In the first shipments released by Mattel the odds were one in six would have the silver earrings. As time passed more and more silver earring dolls started to surface. The silver earrings are still considered to be the harder of the two to find, commanding a higher price. Barbie doll's lightly printed dress is perfect attire for the hot Jamaican weather.

English #4973 • 1991 • $75.00

Barbie doll's riding habit is modernly classic. What else would she want to wear at the Polo Club? I'm glad they didn't have her chasing the fox. At first glance you might think her jacket is made from the same bolt as was Canadian, but no, it's a soft felt and the skirt is a fine poplin.

Italian Reissue #2256 • 1992 • $45.00

This Italian Barbie represents southern Italy. Mattel used a very unusual color combination for this doll that works remarkably well. The new Teresa face mold is used here with terrific teal green eyes. Once again, I want to emphasize how much I like this face mold. I'm not alone on this, collectors continually seek any of the dolls with this mold. Note the box change. These wrap around cello boxes need even more careful handling than most. When lifting these boxes, wrap your fingers around the reinforced cardboard at the bottom. Do not grab the box and squeeze the cello; that will cause it to dent easily. There are two different box styles.

Australian #3626 • 1992 • $45.00

Dressed for the bush and ready to go. Barbie doll rounds up more collectors than cattle in this typical jullaroo outfit. There were two versions of this box, also. The 1992 releases were made in Malaysia and the 1993 releases were made in China and have a red, white, and blue flag and say Special Edition.

Native American #1753 • 1992 • $45.00

Collectors have long been begging Mattel for an American Indian. Finally, the message got through, and when it did, Mattel couldn't stop. There are three to date, and I hope it doesn't stop. Mattel selected the Midge face mold for this fully fringed, suede clothed, beaded dress. Her pitch black hair is typically Native American. Her boots are stitched and styled like the original Eskimo. This doll was so popular that recently Toys Я Us had Mattel reissue her for their stores.

Chinese #11180 • 1993 • $45.00

Mattel chose cherry blossom pink flo-ral satin for Barbie doll's two piece dress. Her little slip-on shoes are perfect for walking the Great Wall you see in the background. Her long black locks are made from the satin strands we box removers love.

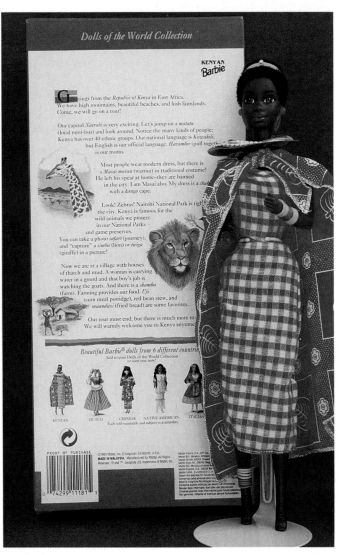

Kenyan #11181 • 1993 • $45.00

Another fantastic doll that belongs in the Dolls of the World series, but looks just as wonderful in the Shani group which started out as a regular line collection. Barbie doll is from East Africa and is wearing a shuka and a kanga cape. This is classic attire for the women of Kenya. This is also the first Barbie doll to have flocked hair!

Dutch #11104 • 1993 • $40.00

Barbie doll looks so clean and crisp in her typical Netherlands outfit. Mattel had made a fashion back in 1964, called Barbie in Holland (see *Barbie Fashions* by Sarah Eames, page 95). The only grievance I heard about this doll was that her shoes weren't wooden. Neither were the ones made back in 1964. I guess if you really want them, you're going to have to carve them yourself.

Native American II #11609 • 1993 • $40.00

More beads, less fringe but longer, lots of feathers. Teresa's face mold... the first American Indian continues to be the favorite to date, but I have a hard time choosing between the two.

International Gift Set I #12043 • 1994 • $125.00

had suggested to Mattel that I would love to see n International gift set...lo and behold, here she . The production of this gift set was limited to ,000 pieces. That's not a lot. By the time this as released, almost everyone had already pur-hased these three dolls separately. Gift sets are lmost always more scarce and generally com-and more money. You investors out there, keep n eye on this one. Keep in mind that it is also e first International gift set.

Irish Reissue #12998 • 1994 • $30.00

Shamrock green is the only choice for Barbie doll's Irish linen party dress. Trimmed with chantilly lace with hat to match, there's no blarney about it... she is terrific!

Polynesian #12700 • 1994 • $40.00

This Polynesian Barbie has what appears to be the tiniest waist I've ever seen. Must be all that wiggling. Barbie doll's historic dance outfit greatly resembles the fashion from 1964 as seen on page 96 in *Barbie Fashion* by Sarah Sink Eames. Her head is adorned with brightly colored tropical flowers.

German Reissue #12698 • 1994 • $30.00

I love the face and hair. (It didn't have to be combed, yeah!) Barbie doll's outfit is the type you'll see at all the tourist attractions when cruising down the Rhine River. Mattel must have had a lot of those ballerina dolls left over that didn't sell; they unfortunately used those white legged bodies up on this collector doll.

American Indian III #12699 • 1995 • $40.00

I was happy to see the Teresa face mold as it suits this American Indian. I love this doll and this grouping within the series, but I don't understand the satin. I have yet to see an authentic Native American dress out of this cloth. I have added all the Pocahontas dolls to my American Indian display. They look fantastic together. These with the New American Heritage series truly make a wonderful display.

International Gift Set II #13939 • 1994 • $95.00

For the second year in a row, Mattel took the existing Dolls of the World and put them in one box. Three dolls in one box take up less space than individually boxed dolls. Space is always a concern. Avid collectors often run out of space before they run out of money.

Royal 1979 • English 1991

Italian 1979 • Italian Reissue 1992

I thought it might be fun to show the originals next to the reissues. Hope you enjoy seeing them together. The first issue is on the left and the reissue is on the right.

Parisian 1979 • Parisian Reissue 1990

Scottish 1980 • Scottish Reissue 1990

Eskimo 1981 • Eskimo Reissue 1990

Spanish 1982 • Spanish Reissue 1991

Irish 1983 • Irish Reissue 1994

German 1986 • German Reissue 1994

Oriental 1980 Variation

Swedish 1983 Variation

Exclusives

Belle• $75.00

Mattel made many dolls for *Beauty and the Beast*. This particular Belle doll was marketed through the Applause company. Belle doll's gown was made from iridescent cello fabric. She was priced for the collector. The box alone was worth it. I wish all my dolls came in the shoe box style. This one is particularly wonderful because it has the window to see Belle's face. This is the only box I have ever seen that doesn't have a copyright date. I asked about it, but no one I talked to had an answer.

Savvy Shopper #12152 • 1994 • $225.00

Nicole Miller designed this luxurious silk printed fabric for this special doll and this special store. This limited edition doll was a delightful surprise for collectors. She follows that great shopping theme that escalated with the release of Madison Avenue for F.A.O. Schwarz (see page 37 of *Barbie Exclusives, book I*). Savvy is a slang derivative from the Spanish word Saber, to know. This is a great doll. I believe she will rival Feeling Groovy (page 13 of *Barbie Exclusives, book I*). Nicole Miller designed this print specifically for Bloomingdale's. The fabric was also made into a limited edition scarf that was sold at the Mattel festival in Florida in 1994. There was supposed to have been a tie available. I never saw one and don't know anyone who ever did. They were cancelled.

vergreen Princess Redhead #13173 • 1994 • $595.00

*vergreen Princess Barbie doll was originally created
a blonde haired doll for the specialty shops (page
of *Barbie Exclusives, Book I*). Mattel participated
the 1994 Walt Disney World Teddy Bear and Doll
onvention. Mattel changed her hair color to red and
e was sold at the convention. She came with a cer-
icate of authenticity. It was limited to 1500 pieces.
hen purchasing this doll it is important that she
ve her paper work with her. You don't want to be
ying a re-root.

Shopping Spree #12749 • 1994 • $35.00

Shopping Spree Barbie doll is the first sportswear customized Barbie doll for F.A.O. Schwarz. She's really cute. I wonder if she goes shopping with the Meijier's Shopping Fun Barbie doll from 1992 (page 56 of *Barbie Exclusives, Book I*). The special little sweatshirt, hat, and bag with F.A.O Schwarz's world famous rocking horse logo is one of the nicest sportswear dolls to date. Barbie doll can get a lot of Polly Pockets in that shopping bag, can't she?

Circus Star #13257 • 1994 • $150.00

ᴀnn Driskill did a fabulous job designing what I would think to be a difficult theme. The colors and fabrics are super. ᴛhe rayon velvet enhances the caliber of this doll and is trimmed with gold from the 1994 Holiday doll. The parasol ᴡas created from the same fabric as we see on the Rainbow doll (page 168). The gold looped trim is the same as the ꜱilver trim on the first American Indian Barbie doll. I've left this doll in the box for this photo because those who ᴀren't fortunate enough to own this doll need to see the expertise of the packers in the Orient. I would never be able to ᴅrape the folds in this cape so magnificently. Ann also did the box cover illustration. This is the first time a Mattel ᴅesigner has had this honor.

Victorian Elegance #12579 • 1994 • $195.00

When Mattel licensed with Hallmark who would have dreamed of the ramifications. Every year we have had more and more collectors coming on board. Victorian Elegance alerted Hallmark collectors to the exciting field of Barbie doll collecting. This and their Christmas ornament sent Hallmark collectors scurrying for matching Holiday Barbie dolls. Many Barbie collectors were caught off guard when they couldn't find the Gold Holiday doll on the shelves of their local store. Victorian Elegance is the first in a series. As Hallmark collectors become more aware and realize how much fun Barbie can be and they continue to participate; until Mattel hires more people and builds more factories, believe me, demand will grow and supplies will not. Unless you order early from specialty shops, be prepared to pay secondary market for almost anything. Ann Driskill designed this first gem for Hallmark.

Polly Pocket #12412 • 1994 • $55.00

Mattel offered through the regular line division Polly Pocket Stacy, Janet, and Whitney. The customized division put this Barbie doll together for Hills. It was a special edition and the number produced was very low. Collectors all over the country were anxious to add her to the grouping. She was difficult to get even if you did have a Hills in your area. Suddenly, she was gone everywhere. Then, just as suddenly, she reappeared. She is very much a favorite with all collectors. It is interesting to note that Mattel utilized the same fabric for the upcoming Russell Stover candies limited edition Barbie doll #14617!

Sea Pearl Mermaid #13940 • 1995 • $35.00

This is the first customized mermaid and another winner for Hills. Barbie doll's opalescent ensemble is trimmed with pearls she dove for herself. Mattel, to date, has released four regular line mermaids in the U.S. and one mermaid for Europe with purple hair.

Night Dazzle #12191 • 1994 • $125.00

J.C. Penney and Ann Driskill must have had a winner here, because she sold out very quickly. Have you been noticing how many dolls now have that great big bow at her waist? There are too many to mention, just flip through our *Barbie Exclusives* books again and see. Mattel chose rich fabric and yet was able to offer this gorgeous doll very reasonably. She could have been packaged in a book box or shoe box and sold for considerably more money. Check out her sister piece on page 170. Both dolls were designed by Mattel's wonderful Ann Driskill!

Fashion Friends Party Dress #7026 • 1990 • $20.00

These K-Mart dolls, by all rights should have been in my other book. I was not aware of them at the time. They are from the customized department and I hoped you would want to see them. There were two variations of this dress. The skirt on the one on the left is from the older Super Star Barbie doll. The one on the right looks suspiciously like Walmart's Frills and Fantasy, but it isn't.

Fashion Friends Swimsuit #7019 • 1990 • $20.00

These nameless dolls were designed and marketed for those whose budget would not permit a genuine Barbie doll. Interestingly, these dolls seem to me to be just as good quality as many regular line dolls. I think of them as being comparable to a My First Barbie doll.

Fashion Friends Pretty Teen #7010 • 1990 • $18.00

If Barbie doll had a friend, then Skipper doll should
too. This no-name doll is wearing something Skippe
doll might have worn.

Silver Sweetheart #12410 • 1994 • $65.00

There are a lot of Sears collectors. This particular doll was to have been for Canada only. Then she turned up in the Sears catalog. Many who called as soon as they got their catalog were told that they were sold out. Back when Sears had a mail-order division it was easy and fun to get Barbie dolls. Now you're going to say to me, you can still order from Sears. Well yes, that's what you would think. But if you inquire when you call the number on your Sears catalog, you will find that it is really Mattel's mail-order division. I almost forgot; if this gown looks familiar to you, it is the same pattern as we saw on Jewel Jubilee, the second wholesale club doll (page 115 of *Barbie Exclusives, Book I*).

City Sophisticate #121005 • 1994 • $155.00

Service Merchandise doesn't exist in my area, so I have never been in one. It must be some classy store to offer such great dolls. This is their fourth and you can see that the fifth is just about as good. If you are one to color coordinate your dolls try her out with the '94 Christmas doll, any of the Summit dolls, Jewel Jubilee, and Satin Nights. Did I point out those luscious green eyes?

Ruby Romance #13612 • 1995 • $65.00

Sometimes I can be so silly. When customers were calling me and asking me to describe this doll, I'd say she's wearing a garnet colored dress. It's ruby! Ruby! Just like her name. Rubies are worth more than garnets. I've got it straight now. Another winner for Service Merchandise. Another winner for you. The art work on the back of this box is fantastic.

Theater Elegance #12077 • 1994 • $200.00

I was very conservative when I ordered this doll for the shop. Her popularity surprised me, but I don't know why, because she was a Geralyn Nelson designed doll, and her dolls as you can see here in the book, are all pretty special. Theater Elegance Barbie doll has borrowed Masquerade Barbie doll's mask. The velvet is the same velvet as on the Nicole Miller doll. The hot pink satin gives her gown life. Barbie doll's earring and necklace are true crystals and the bugle beads on her flower are glass, not plastic. Only the best for Barbie.

Valentine #12675 • 1994 • $45.00

All the Valentine dolls continue to be great sellers. After all, what better gift to give to someone you love than a Valentine and Barbie doll all in one? The Cupids don't show up very well in this photo, but take my word for it, they are darling.

Easter Party #12793 • 1994 • $45.00

Barbie doll had so much Easter fun last year, that she decided to have an Easter party this year. Barbie doll's daffodil yellow flutter sleeves really bring out the chicks on her dress. Those chicks are as happy to get out of their eggs as Barbie doll is to get out of her box. Once again, for the money, this doll is hard to beat.

Holiday Dreams #12192 • 1994 • $45.00

Second of the holiday dolls for the grocery stores and occasionally a drug store, is Holiday Dreams Barbie doll, designed by Heather Dutton. The print on Barbie doll's night shirt has little mice all over. Hiding in the Christmas wreath is the cat. His eyes aren't closed, he's not dreaming, he's screaming about those mice. What's your holiday dream...more Barbie dolls!

Country Western Star #12096 • 1994 • $35.00

This Barbie doll should rightfully have been in the *Barbie Exclusives, Book I.* Unfortunately, my deadline was due at Collector Books and Country Star black Barbie doll had not been released. So, consequently, she didn't make it. Well here she is now. Just having the time of her life country rockin' 'n rollin'.

Country Star Western Horse #12271 • 1994 • $55.00

This isn't a gift set. You don't get the doll, just the horse. I didn't have the heart to leave it out, because they belong together. I really do want to stick with dolls for this book, but sometimes it's hard. This horse was the first all new horse from the customized division. All the other horses to date that were exclusives were leftovers from the international regular line.

Country Bride #13614 • 1994 • $30.00

Wal-Mart must have done well with the count
western theme, because they came back the ne:
year with Country Bride Barbie. Although her bc
date says 1994, she wasn't released till mid 199₄
Well worth the wait! This may be a good time
remind you that the dates are the patent dates c
the boxes, not necessarily the same date as th
doll's release.

Country Bride #13615 • 1994 • $25.00

Barbie's Swiss dot dress is just as sweet as it can be. It is reminiscent of Midge doll's Wedding Day Gift Set from several years prior. The daisies are a nice touch with the pink and white gingham ribbon. If you find one of these loose sometime and you think her veil is cut, it probably isn't. For some bizarre reason, the packers at Mattel tied Barbie up with those twisty ties. In order to accommodate the ties, the veil had to be cut. Why they had to fold her veil up underneath her head beats me. But they did, hence, wrinkles in the illusion, which are difficult to get out.

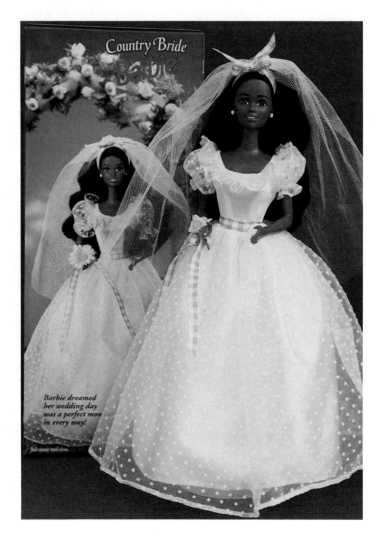

Country Bride #13616 • 1994 • $45.00

Collectors love the Teresa face mold, it started with Rockin' Rappin' Teresa a couple of years earlier. The Hispanic doll to date has been the most scarce. want to thank Helen Vuckovich for getting these dolls for me. There is no Wal-mart here and I'm s busy I can't get out of town to go shopping. This dol was not stocked in all parts of the country.

International Travel #13912 • 1995 • $ 100.00

Barbie doll loves to go. This is not the only time Barbie doll has taken a trip. You'll remember Barbie doll had her suitcases stuffed in the Toys Я Us section. The hat doesn't do much for her, and her float coat resembles those stickers people put on their suitcases when they want everyone to know where they have been. Interestingly, the coat is what makes this doll. It seems to be the same pattern as Madison Avenue Barbie doll's. I think she's a bit overpriced for what you get. There are variations of the bow on the dress and the hat ribbon colors! Some are navy, some hot pink, and some mixed.

Western Stampin' Star Horse Gift Set #5408 • 1990 • $50.00

Western themes keep coming...that's because Mattel knows they sell. Western Stampin' Barbie was sold as a single doll through the regular line division and again in a gift set for the wholesale clubs (see page 132 of *Barbie Exclusives, Book I*). Now if you're paying attention, you might be wondering why it says patented in 1990 when Western Barbie doll wasn't released. I wondered the same thing. Did I have my glasses on when I read the box? Or is it because that's when Star Stepper was patented? This gift set was also shared with Toys Я Us. Once again the box date is not necessarily the same as the doll's patent date.

All American Star Stepper #3712 • 1991 • $65.00

All American Barbie doll with her ever-popular denim western wear is really cute with her elaborately star-studded vest. Mattel used up wet and wild bracelets from the previous year in All Americans Barbie doll's hair. Barbie doll's horse is the first Arabian. Star Stepper could have been purchased separately. His saddlery matches Barbie doll's outfit. The major difference is that Star Stepper isn't wearing Reebok shoes and Barbie doll is. This gift set was also shared with Toy Я Us or visa versa.

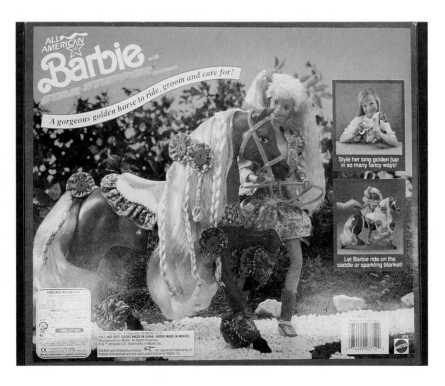

Denim 'N Ruffles #12371 • 1994 • $95.00

This doll was extremely limited. She was only sold as a gift pack with this High Stepper horse. They were merely cello wrapped together. The doll was never offered separately. I'm suspicious that there was manufacturing problems with Barbie doll's hair. It is a fright. I almost had to nail the hat on because the hair is too thick and the hat would not stay.

Bedtime Barbie Gift Set #12184 • 1994 • $45.00

Bedtime Barbie Gift Set comes complete with her bed. This is the only wholesale club doll with foreign writing. She was very limited here in the U.S. as a gift set. This doll in the regular line was a good seller to very young children because she is so soft.

Season's Greetings #12384 • 1994 • $150.00

This is the first in what I hope to be a long running series for the wholesale clubs. These dolls are pretty nice for the money. Collectors seem to really go for anything holiday related. The metallic threads in this doll's festive two-piece suit give sparkle to her eyes. She's a winner in my book and another feather in the cap of Ann Driskill. A small production run was done for Costco stores of Canada. The doll was called Meilleurs Voeux. The dolls in Canada must include French labeling due to the large French-speaking population.

Winter's Eve #13613 • 1994 • $50.00

Personally, I like the face paint on this doll over her predecessor, but I like Season's Greetings Barbie doll's suit more. Then again, this one has fur trim, and I like the fur trim gowns. Which one do you like?

Festival

~ ✦ ~

1994

~ ✦ ~

Nostalgic Brunette Gift Set #12899 • 1994 • $900.00+

Mattel in the fall of 1994, sponsored a once-in-a-life time-event. In commemoration of Barbie doll's 35th birthday, Mattel elected Disney World in Orlando, Florida, to hold the festivities. Mattel offered nine different dolls for sale. Six if them were dolls already on the production line with blonde hair. One of the dolls was all new and two were re-dressed. This Nostalgic Gift Set with brunette hair was limited to 975 pieces. She would become part of a curly-bang trilogy for the avid collector. The unfortunate thing about her was her opening price was $295. That was a lot of money for most spectators, especially those who had come from some distance and had already spent $1500 to attend the party. It was quite a mark up for a set that cost Mattel about $20 to make. Looking back, $295 was cheap!

Barbie Banquet Gift Set Blonde #N/A • $350.00

Banquet night held everyone's attention with guest speakers and wonderful food. The hall was filled with round tables, guests were dressed in formal attire, and most importantly in the center of each table was a large package adorned with streamers and silver ribbon. It did not take long for the word to get out that our dolls were inside those boxes. There were 10 guests to a table and twenty dolls in the box. Each guest would get two dolls. One blonde, one red head.

Barbie Banquet Gift Set Redhead # N/A •
$500.00

Shortly after all had eaten, everyone scrambled to open their dolls. What a lovely surprise. These two would create the curly bang trilogy. She was made to look like the number one Barbie doll from 1959, although there was never a red-headed number one doll until Mattel made the porcelain redhead Gay Parisian in 1991, which also could only be obtained at Disney World. Please remember that you need the Festival sticker and Festival certificate to command this kind of money. There are many re-roots out there. Not shown is a brunette, single-boxed curly-bang doll. Mattel sold these exclusively to Mattel employees. There are rumors these also were to be given to festival attendees or were to have been extra gift set dolls.

Gymnast Brunette #11921 • 1993 • $300.00

Like Dr. Barbie doll there were 1500 of the Gymnast Barbie with brunette hair. You see not all Barbie dolls wear high heels. This flat footed doll is uniquely constructed to bend, move, and pose in all types of positions. She is made of extremely brittle plastic and her joints are cumbersome. Her opening price was $35.00. This is the only Festival doll offered in foreign packaging and she came with extra accessories that the United States version did not have.

Dr. Barbie Brunette #12903 • 1993 • $300.00

Mattel offered two dolls for those on limited budgets. Dr. Barbie doll was one of them. Gymnast Barbie was the other. They were originally offered at $35.00 each. The regular line doll was blonde and came with only one baby. The Festival Dr. Barbie was brunette and had two babies, yet to be named. This brunette was limited to 1500 pieces.

Limited Edition #N/A • 1994 • $550.00

This is the only completely new doll Mattel made for sale expressly for the Festival. Her production level was the highest at 3500 pieces. The reason for this was that she was to have been the banquet gift doll. Someone at Mattel had the good sense to realize that there was a better gift idea, and they switched it to the curly-bang dolls you see on pages 163 and 164. Not that there's anything wrong with this doll, there isn't. She's gorgeous! It's just that the curly nostalgic doll is the doll of the year — her birthday, so it makes more sense. These shoe boxes are great. They are a manageable size, offer easy access to your doll, and help keep her dust-free if you simply put some plastic wrap over the box. This doll has a 22 karat gold Festival stamp on her back, she truly is the official 35th anniversary doll. Mattel's Heather Dutton designed her.

Rainbow #12900 • 1994 • $450.00

This doll was dressed in a fashion that was sold exclusively in the European market. She was limited to 500 pieces. One of three had rooted eyelashes. This Mondrian satin ribbon ball gown is the most colorful of the Festival dolls. Mattel had some fabric left over and used it to create F.A.O. Schwarz's Circus Star Barbie doll's parasol (see page 133). Rainbow's original selling price was $95.00.

Red Velvet Delight #12901 • 1994 • $500.00

This Barbie doll is one of two re-dressed dolls. Kitty Black Perkins originally designed this doll for the Classique Collection. Mattel select-ed another haute couture fashion from the European market, dressed 480 left over black Extravaganza dolls, put her in a silver Festival shoe box, gave her a card of authenticity, and sold her for $95.00.

Night Dazzle Brunette #12907 • 1994 • $550.00

Night Dazzle Barbie doll had been done as a blonde for J.C. Penney (see page 137). The blonde version was not available for very long because 420 of them became Festival dolls with brunette hair. Her pitch black fiber hair is on a black star liner which makes her difficult to see. Her gown is luxurious red moire taffeta with a rich satin velvet overskirt. The floral design is a bit large for her, but as usual Barbie doll pulls it off.

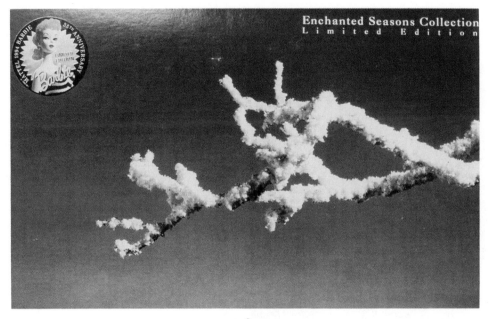

Snow Princess Brunette #12905 • N/A • $2000.00+

Limited to 285 pieces, Snow Princess Barbie doll received a head change for the Festival. For $195.00, opening price, she should have something special, so they gave her the same ornament that was included with the 1989 Holiday doll. A special shelf was added to the box liner for the ornament to rest on. The original blonde had been done for the mail-order division of Mattel. This brunette was the hardest of the Festival dolls to get. Those who really wanted her had to line up the night before. Many slept on concrete outside the building to wait for the doors to open so they could purchase this beauty. I was not willing to sleep on concrete, especially when I had a perfectly good $100.00 room waiting for me. Hence, I don't have one. Bob Gardner has loaned his doll for you to see. Thank you Bob. The festival version also had white legs instead of the tan vinyl legs used for the USA mail-order blonde.

Happy Holidays Brunette #12904 • 1994 • $1,500.00

Only 540 people in the world will ever have a complete collection of holiday dolls. In spite of the shortage for regular line holiday dolls, Mattel surprising
turned this doll into a brunette, added a gorgeous co-
ordinating wreath ornament, gave her the festival se:
and proper authenticity card, and offered her at th
Festival for $250.00. In comparing her to my blond
doll, I discovered that in the bottom left hand corne
where it says "special edition" the scripts are slight
different in style and size, an observation I can on
realize when the boxes are side by side.

Also available from Collector Books

Barbie EXCLUSIVES

Book I
by Margo Rana

#3957 • 8½ x 11 • 160 Pgs. • PB • $18.95

Barbie Exclusives are the prestigious Mattel produced dolls and designs made solely for a company and not sold in any other establishment. These "department store specials" are one of the most sought-after categories of Barbie dolls that Mattel offers. Because it is difficult for the collector to know what is available in different parts of the country, this book is a valuable look at truly harder-to-find dolls, filling a void in this area of Barbie collector's books. With well over 300 gorgeous color photos of Barbie exclusives, it was created to help the collector of customized Barbie dolls to really zero in on his/her personal collection. Dolls are shown with their boxes as well as in vivid close-ups with fantastic details, to assist in identifying played-with dolls. The doll's name and collector value along with interesting facts are given. Featured are department store specials from Sears, Wal-Mart, Service Merchandise, and dolls from more remote stores, porcelain treasures, Disney, and advertising Barbie dolls. This enchanting book includes the newest dolls available and has been anxiously awaited by collectors and dealers.

COLLECTOR BOOKS

Informing Today's Collector

For over two decades we have been keeping collectors informed on trends and values in all fields of antiques and collectibles.

DOLLS, FIGURES & TEDDY BEARS

2382	**Advertising Dolls**, Identification & Values, Robison & Sellers	$9.95
2079	**Barbie** Doll Fashions, Volume I, Eames	$24.95
3957	**Barbie** Exclusives, Rana	$18.95
4557	**Barbie,** The First 30 Years, Deutsch	$24.95
3310	**Black Dolls**, 1820–1991, Perkins	$17.95
3873	**Black Dolls**, Book II, Perkins	$17.95
3810	**Chatty Cathy** Dolls, Lewis	$15.95
2021	Collectible **Action Figures**, 2nd Ed., Manos	$14.95
1529	Collector's Encyclopedia of **Barbie** Dolls, DeWein	$19.95
4506	Collector's Guide to **Dolls in Uniform**, Bourgeois	$18.95
3727	Collector's Guide to **Ideal Dolls**, Izen	$18.95
3728	Collector's Guide to Miniature **Teddy Bears**, Powell	$17.95
3967	Collector's Guide to **Trolls**, Peterson	$19.95
4569	**Howdy Doody,** Collector's Reference and Trivia Guide, Koch	$16.95
1067	**Madame Alexander** Dolls, Smith	$19.95
3971	**Madame Alexander** Dolls Price Guide #20, Smith	$9.95
3733	**Modern Collector's** Dolls, Sixth Series, Smith	$24.95
3991	**Modern Collector's** Dolls, Seventh Series, Smith	$24.95
4571	**Liddle Kiddles**, Identification & Value Guide, Langford	$18.95
3972	Patricia Smith's **Doll Values**, Antique to Modern, 11th Edition	$12.95
3826	Story of **Barbie**, Westenhouser	$19.95
1513	**Teddy Bears & Steiff** Animals, Mandel	$9.95
1817	**Teddy Bears & Steiff** Animals, 2nd Series, Mandel	$19.95
2084	**Teddy Bears, Annalee's & Steiff** Animals, 3rd Series, Mandel	$19.95
1808	Wonder of **Barbie**, Manos	$9.95
1430	World of **Barbie** Dolls, Manos	$9.95

FURNITURE

1457	American **Oak** Furniture, McNerney	$9.95
3716	American **Oak** Furniture, Book II, McNerney	$12.95
1118	Antique **Oak** Furniture, Hill	$7.95
2132	Collector's Encyclopedia of **American** Furniture, Vol. I, Swedberg	$24.95
2271	Collector's Encyclopedia of **American** Furniture, Vol. II, Swedberg	$24.95
3720	Collector's Encyclopedia of **American** Furniture, Vol. III, Swedberg	$24.95
1437	Collector's Guide to **Country** Furniture, Raycraft	$9.95
3878	Collector's Guide to **Oak** Furniture, George	$12.95
1755	Furniture of the **Depression Era**, Swedberg	$19.95
3906	**Heywood-Wakefield** Modern Furniture, Rouland	$18.95
1965	**Pine** Furniture, Our American Heritage, McNerney	$14.95
1885	**Victorian** Furniture, Our American Heritage, McNerney	$9.95
3829	**Victorian** Furniture, Our American Heritage, Book II, McNerney	$9.95
3869	**Victorian** Furniture books, 2 volume set, McNerney	$19.90

JEWELRY, HATPINS, WATCHES & PURSES

1712	Antique & Collector's **Thimbles** & Accessories, Mathis	$19.95
1748	Antique **Purses**, Revised Second Ed., Holiner	$19.95
1278	Art Nouveau & Art Deco **Jewelry**, Baker	$9.95
4558	**Christmas** Pins, Past and Present, Gallina	$18.95
3875	Collecting Antique **Stickpins**, Kerins	$16.95
3722	Collector's Ency. of **Compacts, Carryalls & Face Powder Boxes**, Mueller	$24.95
3992	Complete Price Guide to **Watches**, #15, Shugart	$21.95
1716	Fifty Years of Collectible **Fashion Jewelry**, 1925-1975, Baker	$19.95
1424	**Hatpins** & Hatpin Holders, Baker	$9.95
4570	Ladies' **Compacts**, Gerson	$24.95
1181	100 Years of Collectible **Jewelry**, 1850-1950, Baker	$9.95
2348	20th Century Fashionable Plastic **Jewelry**, Baker	$19.95
3830	Vintage **Vanity Bags & Purses**, Gerson	$24.95

TOYS, MARBLES & CHRISTMAS COLLECTIBLES

3427	**Advertising Character** Collectibles, Dotz	$17.95
2333	Antique & Collector's **Marbles**, 3rd Ed., Grist	$9.95
3827	Antique & Collector's **Toys**, 1870–1950, Longest	$24.95
3956	Baby Boomer **Games**, Identification & Value Guide, Polizzi	$24.95
3717	**Christmas** Collectibles, 2nd Edition, Whitmyer	$24.95
1752	**Christmas** Ornaments, Lights & Decorations, Johnson	$19.95
3874	Collectible Coca-Cola Toy **Trucks**, deCourtivron	$24.95
2338	Collector's Encyclopedia of **Disneyana**, Longest, Stern	$24.95
2151	Collector's Guide to **Tootsietoys**, 2nd Ed., Richter	$16.95
3436	Grist's Big Book of **Marbles**	$19.95
3970	Grist's Machine-Made & Contemporary **Marbles**, 2nd Ed.	$9.95
3732	**Matchbox®** Toys, 1948 to 1993, Johnson	$18.95
3823	**Mego** Toys, An Illustrated Value Guide, Chrouch	15.95
1540	**Modern Toys** 1930–1980, Baker	$19.95
3888	**Motorcycle** Toys, Antique & Contemporary, Gentry/Downs	$18.95
3891	Schroeder's Collectible **Toys**, Antique to Modern Price Guide, 2nd Ed.	$17.95
1886	Stern's Guide to **Disney** Collectibles	$14.95
2139	Stern's Guide to **Disney** Collectibles, 2nd Series	$14.95
3975	Stern's Guide to **Disney** Collectibles, 3rd Series	$18.95
2028	**Toys**, Antique & Collectible, Longest	$14.95
3975	**Zany Characters** of the Ad World, Lamphier	$16.95

INDIANS, GUNS, KNIVES, TOOLS, PRIMITIVES

1868	Antique **Tools,** Our American Heritage, McNerney	$9.95
2015	Archaic **Indian** Points & Knives, Edler	$14.95
1426	**Arrowheads** & Projectile Points, Hothem	$7.95
2279	**Indian** Artifacts of the Midwest, Hothem	$14.95
3885	**Indian** Artifacts of the Midwest, Book II, Hothem	$16.95
1964	**Indian** Axes & Related Stone Artifacts, Hothem	$14.95
2023	**Keen Kutter** Collectibles, Heuring	$14.95
3887	Modern **Guns**, Identification & Values, 10th Ed., Quertermous	$12.95
4505	Standard Guide to **Razors**, Ritchie & Stewart	$9.95
3325	Standard **Knife** Collector's Guide, 2nd Ed., Ritchie & Stewart	$12.95

PAPER COLLECTIBLES & BOOKS

1441	Collector's Guide to **Post Cards**, Wood	$9.95
2081	Guide to Collecting **Cookbooks**, Allen	$14.95
3969	Huxford's **Old Book** Value Guide, 7th Ed.	$19.95
3821	Huxford's **Paperback** Value Guide	$19.95
2080	Price Guide to **Cookbooks & Recipe Leaflets**, Dickinson	$9.95
2346	**Sheet Music** Reference & Price Guide, 2nd Ed., Pafik & Guiheen	$18.95

GLASSWARE

1006	**Cambridge Glass** Reprint 1930–1934	$14.95
1007	**Cambridge Glass** Reprint 1949–1953	$14.95
2310	**Children's Glass Dishes**, China & Furniture, Vol. I, Lechler	$19.95
1627	**Children's Glass Dishes**, China & Furniture, Vol. II, Lechler	$19.95
4561	Collectible **Drinking Glasses**, Chase & Kelly	$17.95
3719	Coll. **Glassware** from the 40's, 50's & 60's, 3rd Ed., Florence	$19.95
2352	Collector's Encyclopedia of **Akro Agate Glassware**, Florence	$14.95
1810	Collector's Encyclopedia of **American Art Glass**, Shuman	$29.95
3312	Collector's Encyclopedia of **Children's Dishes**, Whitmyer	$19.95
3724	Collector's Encyclopedia of **Depression Glass**, 12th Ed., Florence	$19.95
1664	Collector's Encyclopedia of **Heisey Glass**, 1925–1938, Bredehoft	$24.95
3905	Collector's Encyclopedia of **Milk Glass**, Newbound	$24.95
1523	Colors In **Cambridge Glass**, National Cambridge Soceity	$19.95

COLLECTOR BOOKS
Informing Today's Collector

564	**Crackle Glass**, Weitman	$18.95
275	**Czechoslovakian Glass** and Collectibles, Barta	$16.95
882	**Elegant Glassware** of the Depression Era, 6th Ed., Florence	$19.95
380	Encyclopedia of **Pattern Glass**, McClain	$12.95
981	Ever's Standard **Cut Glass** Value Guide	$12.95
725	**Fostoria**, Pressed, Blown & Hand Molded Shapes, Kerr	$24.95
883	**Fostoria Stemware**, The Crystal for America, Long & Seate	$24.95
318	**Glass Animals** of the Depression Era, Garmon & Spencer	$19.95
886	**Kitchen Glassware** of the Depression Years, 5th Ed., Florence	$19.95
394	**Oil Lamps II**, Glass Kerosene Lamps, Thuro	$24.95
889	Pocket Guide to **Depression Glass**, 9th Ed., Florence	$9.95
739	Standard Encyclopedia of **Carnival Glass**, 4th Ed., Edwards	$24.95
740	Standard **Carnival Glass** Price Guide, 9th Ed.	$9.95
974	Standard Encyclopedia of **Opalescent Glass**, Edwards	$19.95
848	**Very Rare Glassware** of the Depression Years, Florence	$24.95
140	**Very Rare Glassware** of the Depression Years, 2nd Series, Florence	$24.95
326	**Very Rare Glassware** of the Depression Years, 3rd Series, Florence	$24.95
909	**Very Rare Glassware** of the Depression Years, 4th Series, Florence	$24.95
224	World of **Salt Shakers**, 2nd Ed., Lechner	$24.95

POTTERY

312	**Blue & White Stoneware**, McNerney	$9.95
958	So. Potteries **Blue Ridge Dinnerware**, 3rd Ed., Newbound	$14.95
959	**Blue Willow**, 2nd Ed., Gaston	$14.95
816	Collectible **Vernon Kilns**, Nelson	$24.95
311	Collecting **Yellow Ware** – Id. & Value Guide, McAllister	$16.95
373	Collector's Encyclopedia of **American Dinnerware**, Cunningham	$24.95
815	Collector's Encyclopedia of **Blue Ridge Dinnerware**, Newbound	$19.95
272	Collector's Encyclopedia of **California Pottery**, Chipman	$24.95
811	Collector's Encyclopedia of **Colorado Pottery**, Carlton	$24.95
133	Collector's Encyclopedia of **Cookie Jars**, Roerig	$24.95
723	Collector's Encyclopedia of **Cookie Jars**, Volume II, Roerig	$24.95
429	Collector's Encyclopedia of **Cowan Pottery**, Saloff	$24.95
209	Collector's Encyclopedia of **Fiesta**, 7th Ed., Huxford	$19.95
961	Collector's Encyclopedia of **Early Noritake**, Alden	$24.95
439	Collector's Encyclopedia of **Flow Blue China**, Gaston	$19.95
812	Collector's Encyclopedia of **Flow Blue China**, 2nd Ed., Gaston	$24.95
813	Collector's Encyclopedia of **Hall China**, 2nd Ed., Whitmyer	$24.95
431	Collector's Encyclopedia of **Homer Laughlin China**, Jasper	$24.95
276	Collector's Encyclopedia of **Hull Pottery**, Roberts	$19.95
573	Collector's Encyclopedia of **Knowles, Taylor & Knowles**, Gaston	$24.95
962	Collector's Encyclopedia of **Lefton China**, DeLozier	$19.95
210	Collector's Encyclopedia of **Limoges Porcelain**, 2nd Ed., Gaston	$24.95
334	Collector's Encyclopedia of **Majolica Pottery**, Katz-Marks	$19.95
358	Collector's Encyclopedia of **McCoy Pottery**, Huxford	$19.95
963	Collector's Encyclopedia of **Metlox Potteries**, Gibbs Jr.	$24.95
313	Collector's Encyclopedia of **Niloak**, Gifford	$19.95
837	Collector's Encyclopedia of **Nippon Porcelain I**, Van Patten	$24.95
1089	Collector's Ency. of **Nippon Porcelain**, 2nd Series, Van Patten	$24.95
1665	Collector's Ency. of **Nippon Porcelain**, 3rd Series, Van Patten	$24.95
1836	**Nippon Porcelain** Price Guide, Van Patten	$9.95
447	Collector's Encyclopedia of **Noritake**, Van Patten	$19.95
1432	Collector's Encyclopedia of **Noritake**, 2nd Series, Van Patten	$24.95
1037	Collector's Encyclopedia of **Occupied Japan**, Vol. I, Florence	$14.95
1038	Collector's Encyclopedia of **Occupied Japan**, Vol. II, Florence	$14.95
2088	Collector's Encyclopedia of **Occupied Japan**, Vol. III, Florence	$14.95
1019	Collector's Encyclopedia of **Occupied Japan**, Vol. IV, Florence	$14.95
2335	Collector's Encyclopedia of **Occupied Japan**, Vol. V, Florence	$14.95
1964	Collector's Encyclopedia of **Pickard China**, Reed	$24.95
1311	Collector's Encyclopedia of **R.S. Prussia**, 1st Series, Gaston	$24.95
1715	Collector's Encyclopedia of **R.S. Prussia**, 2nd Series, Gaston	$24.95
1726	Collector's Encyclopedia of **R.S. Prussia**, 3rd Series, Gaston	$24.95
3877	Collector's Encyclopedia of **R.S. Prussia**, 4th Series, Gaston	$24.95
1034	Collector's Encyclopedia of **Roseville Pottery**, Huxford	$19.95
1035	Collector's Encyclopedia of **Roseville Pottery**, 2nd Ed., Huxford	$19.95
1357	**Roseville** Price Guide No. 10	$9.95
2083	Collector's Encyclopedia of **Russel Wright** Designs, Kerr	$19.95
3965	Collector's Encyclopedia of **Sascha Brastoff**, Conti, Bethany & Seay	$24.95

3314	Collector's Encyclopedia of **Van Briggle** Art Pottery, Sasicki	$24.95
2111	Collector's Encyclopedia of **Weller Pottery**, Huxford	$29.95
3452	Coll. Guide to Country Stoneware & Pottery, Raycraft	$11.95
2077	Coll. Guide to **Country Stoneware & Pottery**, 2nd Series, Raycraft	$14.95
3433	Collector's Guide To **Harker Pottery** - U.S.A., Colbert	$17.95
3434	Coll. Guide to **Hull Pottery**, The Dinnerware Line, Gick-Burke	$16.95
3876	Collector's Guide to **Lu-Ray Pastels**, Meehan	$18.95
3814	Collector's Guide to **Made in Japan** Ceramics, White	$18.95
4565	Collector's Guide to **Rockingham**, The Enduring Ware, Brewer	$14.95
2339	Collector's Guide to **Shawnee Pottery**, Vanderbilt	$19.95
1425	**Cookie Jars**, Westfall	$9.95
3440	**Cookie Jars**, Book II, Westfall	$19.95
3435	Debolt's Dictionary of **American Pottery Marks**	$17.95
2379	Lehner's Ency. of **U.S. Marks** on Pottery, Porcelain & China	$24.95
3825	**Puritan Pottery**, Morris	$24.95
1670	**Red Wing Collectibles**, DePasquale	$9.95
1440	**Red Wing Stoneware**, DePasquale	$9.95
3738	**Shawnee Pottery**, Mangus	$24.95
3327	**Watt Pottery** – Identification & Value Guide, Morris	$19.95

OTHER COLLECTIBLES

2269	Antique **Brass & Copper** Collectibles, Gaston	$16.95
1880	Antique **Iron**, McNerney	$9.95
3872	Antique **Tins**, Dodge	$24.95
1714	**Black** Collectibles, Gibbs	$19.95
1128	**Bottle** Pricing Guide, 3rd Ed., Cleveland	$7.95
3959	**Cereal Box** Bonanza, The 1950's, Bruce	$19.95
3718	Collectible **Aluminum**, Grist	$16.95
3445	Collectible **Cats**, An Identification & Value Guide, Fyke	$18.95
4560	Collectible **Cats**, An Identification & Value Guide, Book II, Fyke	$19.95
4563	Collector's Encyclopedia of **Wall Pockets**, Newbound	$19.95
1634	Collector's Ency. of Figural & Novelty **Salt & Pepper Shakers**, Davern	$19.95
2020	Collector's Ency. of Figural & Novelty **Salt & Pepper Shakers**, Vol. II, Davern	$19.95
2018	Collector's Encyclopedia of **Granite Ware**, Greguire	$24.95
3430	Collector's Encyclopedia of **Granite Ware**, Book II, Greguire	$24.95
3879	Collector's Guide to **Antique Radios**, 3rd Ed., Bunis	$18.95
1916	Collector's Guide to **Art Deco**, Gaston	$14.95
3880	Collector's Guide to **Cigarette Lighters**, Flanagan	$17.95
1537	Collector's Guide to **Country Baskets**, Raycraft	$9.95
3966	Collector's Guide to **Inkwells**, Identification & Values, Badders	$18.95
3881	Collector's Guide to **Novelty Radios**, Bunis/Breed	$18.95
3729	Collector's Guide to **Snow Domes**, Guarnaccia	$18.95
3730	Collector's Guide to **Transistor Radios**, Bunis	$15.95
2276	**Decoys**, Kangas	$24.95
1629	**Doorstops**, Identification & Values, Bertoia	$9.95
4567	Figural **Napkin Rings**, Gottschalk & Whitson	$18.95
3968	**Fishing Lure** Collectibles, Murphy/Edmisten	$24.95
3817	**Flea Market Trader**, 10th Ed., Huxford	$12.95
3976	Foremost Guide to **Uncle Sam** Collectibles, Czulewicz	$24.95
3819	**General Store Collectibles**, Wilson	$24.95
2215	Goldstein's **Coca-Cola** Collectibles	$16.95
3884	Huxford's Collectible **Advertising**, 2nd Ed.	$24.95
2216	**Kitchen Antiques**, 1790–1940, McNerney	$14.95
3321	Ornamental & Figural **Nutcrackers**, Rittenhouse	$16.95
2026	**Railroad** Collectibles, 4th Ed., Baker	$14.95
1632	**Salt & Pepper Shakers**, Guarnaccia	$9.95
1888	**Salt & Pepper Shakers** II, Identification & Value Guide, Book II, Guarnaccia	$14.95
2220	**Salt & Pepper Shakers** III, Guarnaccia	$14.95
3443	**Salt & Pepper Shakers** IV, Guarnaccia	$18.95
4555	**Schroeder's Antiques Price Guide**, 14th Ed., Huxford	$14.95
2096	**Silverplated Flatware**, Revised 4th Edition, Hagan	$14.95
1922	Standard **Old Bottle** Price Guide, Sellari	$14.95
3892	**Toy & Miniature Sewing Machines**, Thomas	$18.95
3828	Value Guide to **Advertising Memorabilia**, Summers	$18.95
3977	Value Guide to **Gas Station** Memorabilia, Summers & Priddy	$24.95
4572	**Wall Pockets** of the Past, Perkins	$17.95
3444	**Wanted to Buy**, 5th Edition	$9.95

Schroeder's
ANTIQUES
Price Guide

. . . is the #1 best-selling antiques & collectibles value guide on the market today, and here's why . . .

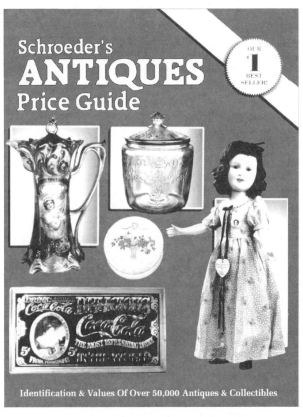

Schroeder's ANTIQUES Price Guide

OUR #1 BEST SELLER!

Identification & Values Of Over 50,000 Antiques & Collectibles

8½ x 11, 608 Pages, $14.95

• *More than 300 advisors, well-known dealers, and top-notch collectors work together with our editors to bring you accurate information regarding pricing and identification.*

• *More than 45,000 items in almost 500 categories are listed along with hundreds of sharp original photos that illustrate not only the rare and unusual, but the common, popular collectibles as well.*

• *Each large close-up shot shows important details clearly. Every subject is represented with histories and background information, a feature not found in any of our competitors' publications.*

• *Our editors keep abreast of newly developing trends, often adding several new categories a year as the need arises.*

If it merits the interest of today's collector, you'll find it in *Schroeder's*. And you can feel confident that the information we publish is up to date and accurate. Our advisors thoroughly check each category to spot inconsistencies, listings that may not be entirely reflective of market dealings, and lines too vague to be of merit. Only the best of the lot remains for publication.

Without doubt, you'll find
SCHROEDER'S ANTIQUES PRICE GUIDE
the only one to buy for
reliable information and values.

COLLECTOR BOOKS
A Division of Schroeder Publishing Co., Inc.